LA LA LAND

FOR PIANO SOLO

MUSIC FROM THE MOTION PICTURE SOUNDTRACK

ISBN 978-1-5400-3590-5

HAL•LEONARD®

For all works contained herein:
Unauthorized copying, arranging, adapting, recording, internet posting, public performance, or other distribution of the music in this publication is an infringement of copyright.
Infringers are liable under the law.

Visit Hal Leonard Online at
www.halleonard.com

World headquarters, contact:
Hal Leonard
7777 West Bluemound Road
Milwaukee, WI 53213
Email: info@halleonard.com

In Europe, contact:
Hal Leonard Europe Limited
1 Red Place
London, W1K 6PL
Email: info@halleonardeurope.com

In Australia, contact:
Hal Leonard Australia Pty. Ltd.
4 Lentara Court
Cheltenham, Victoria, 3192 Australia
Email: info@halleonard.com.au

4 ANOTHER DAY OF SUN

8 SOMEONE IN THE CROWD

12 MIA & SEBASTIAN'S THEME

18 A LOVELY NIGHT

15 CITY OF STARS

22 PLANETARIUM

29 START A FIRE

32 ENGAGEMENT PARTY

34 AUDITION
(THE FOOLS WHO DREAM)

38 EPILOGUE

ANOTHER DAY OF SUN

Music by JUSTIN HURWITZ
Lyrics by BENJ PASEK & JUSTIN PAUL

© 2016 Justin Hurwitz Music (BMI), Warner-Tamerlane Publishing Corp. (BMI), administered by Warner-Tamerlane Publishing Corp. (BMI),
B Lion Music (BMI), administered by Songs Of Universal, Inc. (BMI)/ Pick In A Pinch Music (ASCAP), breathelike music (ASCAP),
WB Music Corp. (ASCAP) administered by WB Music Corp. (ASCAP), and A Lion Music (ASCAP), administered by Universal Music Corp. (ASCAP)
This arrangement © 2019 Justin Hurwitz Music (BMI), Warner-Tamerlane Publishing Corp. (BMI), administered by Warner-Tamerlane Publishing Corp. (BMI),
B Lion Music (BMI), administered by Songs Of Universal, Inc. (BMI)/ Pick In A Pinch Music (ASCAP), breathelike music (ASCAP),
WB Music Corp. (ASCAP) administered by WB Music Corp. (ASCAP), and A Lion Music (ASCAP), administered by Universal Music Corp. (ASCAP)
All Rights Reserved Used by Permission

21
25
30
35
40

45
49
f
53
57
61

65
69
73
f
78
1.
2.
83
mp
ff
8va

SOMEONE IN THE CROWD

Music by JUSTIN HURWITZ
Lyrics by BENJ PASEK & JUSTIN PAUL

© 2016 Justin Hurwitz Music (BMI), Warner-Tamerlane Publishing Corp. (BMI), administered by Warner-Tamerlane Publishing Corp. (BMI), and
B Lion Music (BMI) administered by Songs Of Universal, Inc. (BMI)/
Pick In A Pinch Music (ASCAP), breathelike music (ASCAP), WB Music Corp. (ASCAP) administered by WB Music Corp. (ASCAP) and
A Lion Music (ASCAP) administered by Universal Music Corp. (ASCAP)
This arrangement © 2019 Justin Hurwitz Music (BMI), Warner-Tamerlane Publishing Corp. (BMI), administered by Warner-Tamerlane Publishing Corp. (BMI), and
B Lion Music (BMI) administered by Songs Of Universal, Inc. (BMI)/
Pick In A Pinch Music (ASCAP), breathelike music (ASCAP), WB Music Corp. (ASCAP) administered by WB Music Corp. (ASCAP) and
A Lion Music (ASCAP) administered by Universal Music Corp. (ASCAP)
All Rights Reserved Used by Permission

21
simile
25
30
p
mf
35
40

45
49
f
53
57
61
66
molto rit.

71
Slowly and freely
mp
With pedal
rit.
75
Slowly, in time
mp
molto accel. e cresc.
(no pedal)
79
Tempo Primo
f
simile
83
87
92
ff

MIA & SEBASTIAN'S THEME

Music by
JUSTIN HURWITZ

© 2016 B Lion Music (BMI) administered by Songs Of Universal, Inc. (BMI)/Warner-Tamerlane Publishing Corp. (BMI)
This arrangement © 2019 B Lion Music (BMI) administered by Songs Of Universal, Inc. (BMI)/Warner-Tamerlane Publishing Corp. (BMI)
All Rights Reserved Used by Permission

21
26
cresc. e accel.
30
34
As fast as possible, freely
8va
rit.
f
3
37
(8va)
8va

40
8va
42
(8va)
45
48
8va
rit.
52
Fast
8va

CITY OF STARS

Music by JUSTIN HURWITZ
Lyrics by BENJ PASEK & JUSTIN PAUL

© 2016 Justin Hurwitz Music (BMI), Warner-Tamerlane Publishing Corp. (BMI), administered by Warner-Tamerlane Publishing Corp. (BMI)/
B Lion Music (BMI), administered by Songs Of Universal, Inc. (BMI)/
Pick In A Pinch Music (ASCAP), breathelike music (ASCAP), WB Music Corp. (ASCAP), administered by WB Music Corp. (ASCAP)/
A Lion Music (ASCAP), administered by Universal Music Corp. (ASCAP)
This arrangement © 2019 Justin Hurwitz Music (BMI), Warner-Tamerlane Publishing Corp. (BMI), administered by Warner-Tamerlane Publishing Corp. (BMI)/
B Lion Music (BMI), administered by Songs Of Universal, Inc. (BMI)/
Pick In A Pinch Music (ASCAP), breathelike music (ASCAP), WB Music Corp. (ASCAP), administered by WB Music Corp. (ASCAP)/
A Lion Music (ASCAP), administered by Universal Music Corp. (ASCAP)
All Rights Reserved Used by Permission

21
mp
25
29
3
33
mf
37

41
45
49
freely
mp a tempo
53
57
freely
a tempo
rit.
p

A LOVELY NIGHT

Music by JUSTIN HURWITZ
Lyrics by BENJ PASEK & JUSTIN PAUL

© 2016 Justin Hurwitz Music (BMI), Warner-Tamerlane Publishing Corp. (BMI), administered by Warner-Tamerlane Publishing Corp. (BMI),
and B Lion Music (BMI) administered by Songs Of Universal, Inc. (BMI)/Pick In A Pinch Music (ASCAP), breathelike music (ASCAP),
WB Music Corp. (ASCAP) administered by WB Music Corp. (ASCAP) and A Lion Music (ASCAP) administered by Universal Music Corp. (ASCAP)
This arrangement © 2019 Justin Hurwitz Music (BMI), Warner-Tamerlane Publishing Corp. (BMI), administered by Warner-Tamerlane Publishing Corp. (BMI),
and B Lion Music (BMI) administered by Songs Of Universal, Inc. (BMI)/Pick In A Pinch Music (ASCAP), breathelike music (ASCAP),
WB Music Corp. (ASCAP) administered by WB Music Corp. (ASCAP) and A Lion Music (ASCAP) administered by Universal Music Corp. (ASCAP)
All Rights Reserved Used by Permission

16
20
24
28
f
mp delicately
32

36
f
39
42
46
50
rit.

54
Faster, straight 8ths
mp
f
legato
59
63
mf
legato
67
3
rit.
71
Moderate Swing
p

PLANETARIUM

Music by
JUSTIN HURWITZ

© 2016 B Lion Music (BMI) administered by Songs Of Universal, Inc. (BMI)/Warner-Tamerlane Publishing Corp. (BMI)
This arrangement © 2019 B Lion Music (BMI) administered by Songs Of Universal, Inc. (BMI)/Warner-Tamerlane Publishing Corp. (BMI)
All Rights Reserved Used by Permission

22
8va
tr
26
32
37
Slightly faster
43

48
53
58
63
68

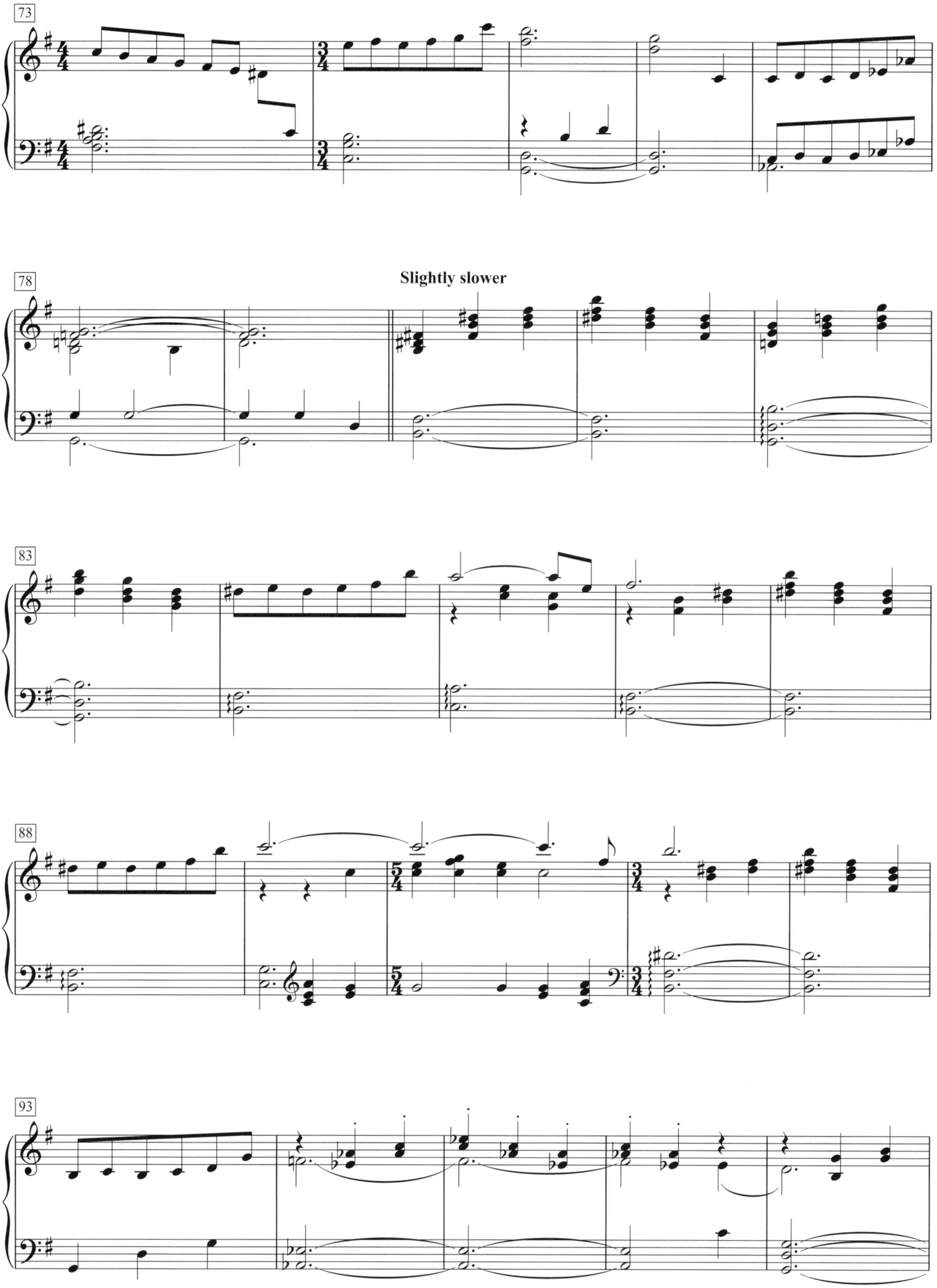
73
78
Slightly slower
83
88
93

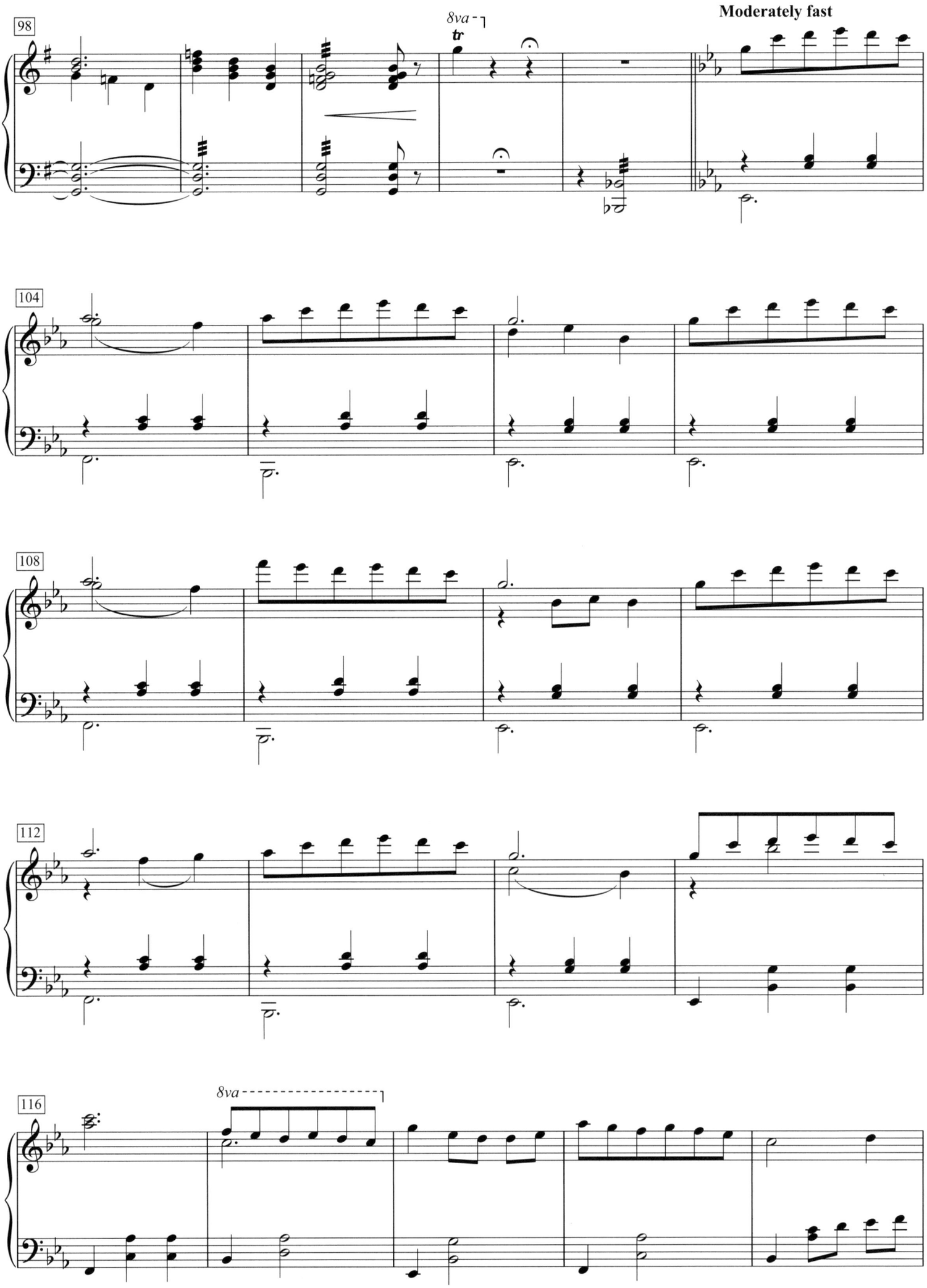
98
8va
tr
Moderately fast
104
108
112
116
8va

121
125
130
136
144
3
3

151
156
163
molto rit.
170
Moderately slow
175
8va

START A FIRE

Music & Lyrics by JOHN STEPHENS,
ANGÉLIQUE CINÉLU, MARIUS DE VRIES
and JUSTIN HURWITZ

© 2016 John Legend Publishing (BMI) administered by BMG Rights Management (US) LLC (BMI)/Joanie's Girl Publishing (BMI)/Blue Barn Music (PRS/ASCAP) and WB Music Corp. (ASCAP), all administered by WB Music Corp. (ASCAP)/ Justin Hurwitz Music (BMI) and Warner-Tamerlane Publishing Corp. (BMI), all administered by Warner-Tamerlane Publishing Corp. (BMI)/ B Lion Music (BMI), administered by Songs Of Universal, Inc. (BMI)/A Lion Music (ASCAP), administered by Universal Music Corp. (ASCAP)
This arrangement © 2019 John Legend Publishing (BMI) administered by BMG Rights Management (US) LLC (BMI)/Joanie's Girl Publishing (BMI)/ Blue Barn Music (PRS/ASCAP) and WB Music Corp. (ASCAP), all administered by WB Music Corp. (ASCAP)/Justin Hurwitz Music (BMI) and Warner-Tamerlane Publishing Corp. (BMI), all administered by Warner-Tamerlane Publishing Corp. (BMI)/ B Lion Music (BMI), administered by Songs Of Universal, Inc. (BMI)/A Lion Music (ASCAP), administered by Universal Music Corp. (ASCAP)
All Rights Reserved Used by Permission

12
15
18
21
25

29
f
32
mf
35
39
f
42
ff

ENGAGEMENT PARTY

Music by
JUSTIN HURWITZ

© 2016 B Lion Music (BMI) administered by Songs Of Universal, Inc. (BMI)/Warner-Tamerlane Publishing Corp. (BMI)
This arrangement © 2019 B Lion Music (BMI) administered by Songs Of Universal, Inc. (BMI)/Warner-Tamerlane Publishing Corp. (BMI)
All Rights Reserved Used by Permission

16
19
23
26
29
rit.

AUDITION
(The Fools Who Dream)

Music by JUSTIN HURWITZ
Lyrics by BENJ PASEK and JUSTIN PAUL

© 2016 Justin Hurwitz Music (BMI), Warner-Tamerlane Publishing Corp. (BMI), administered by Warner-Tamerlane Publishing Corp. (BMI)/
B Lion Music (BMI), administered by Songs Of Universal, Inc. (BMI)/Pick In A Pinch Music (ASCAP), breathelike music (ASCAP),
WB Music Corp. (ASCAP), administered by WB Music Corp. (ASCAP)/A Lion Music (ASCAP), administered by Universal Music Corp. (ASCAP)
This arrangement © 2019 Justin Hurwitz Music (BMI), Warner-Tamerlane Publishing Corp. (BMI), administered by Warner-Tamerlane Publishing Corp. (BMI)/
B Lion Music (BMI), administered by Songs Of Universal, Inc. (BMI)/ Pick In A Pinch Music (ASCAP), breathelike music (ASCAP),
WB Music Corp. (ASCAP), administered by WB Music Corp. (ASCAP)/A Lion Music (ASCAP), administered by Universal Music Corp. (ASCAP)
All Rights Reserved Used by Permission

30
Faster
3
5
mp
35
40
45
51

57
62
accel. e cresc.
Più mosso
mf
68
73
78
poco rit.
83
Broadening
f

88
rall.
93
98
103
rit. e dim.
Slower, with freedom
mp
109
L.H.
3
114
pp

EPILOGUE

Music by
JUSTIN HURWITZ

© 2016 B Lion Music (BMI) administered by Songs Of Universal, Inc. (BMI)/Warner-Tamerlane Publishing Corp. (BMI)
This arrangement © 2019 B Lion Music (BMI) administered by Songs Of Universal, Inc. (BMI)/Warner-Tamerlane Publishing Corp. (BMI)
All Rights Reserved Used by Permission

21
25
Moderately fast, in 2
mf
30
35
40
Swing

45
50
55
60
65
71

76
81
Moderately, expressively (♩♩ = ♩♩)
85
8va
p sub.
Slightly faster
89
mp
94
accel.
99
Moderately fast Swing (♩♩ = ♩♪)
mf

103
107
111
115
120

124
Moderately fast (♫ = ♫)
mf
128
133
rall.
138
142
Slightly slower, broadly
f

146
150
155
161
166
p cresc.
ff
173 Moderately (♩♩ = ♩♪)
p

177
181
185
3
189
3
rit.
Slowly, very freely (♫ = ♫)
193
pp decresc. to end
198
1.
2.

YOUR FAVORITE MUSIC ARRANGED FOR PIANO SOLO

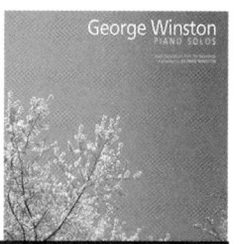

ARTIST, COMPOSER, TV & MOVIE SONGBOOKS

Adele for Piano Solo – 3rd Edition
00820186 ..... $19.99

The Beatles Piano Solo
00294023 ..... $17.99

A Charlie Brown Christmas
00313176 ..... $19.99

Paul Cardall – The Hymns Collection
00295925 ..... $24.99

Coldplay for Piano Solo
00307637 ..... $17.99

Selections from Final Fantasy
00148699 ..... $19.99

Alexis Ffrench – The Sheet Music Collection
00345258 ..... $19.99

Game of Thrones
00199166 ..... $19.99

Hamilton
00354612 ..... $19.99

Hillsong Worship Favorites
00303164 ..... $14.99

How to Train Your Dragon
00138210 ..... $22.99

Elton John Collection
00306040 ..... $24.99

La La Land
00283691 ..... $16.99

John Legend Collection
00233195 ..... $17.99

Les Misérables
00290271 ..... $22.99

Little Women
00338470 ..... $19.99

Outlander: The Series
00254460 ..... $19.99

The Peanuts® Illustrated Songbook
00313178 ..... $29.99

Astor Piazzolla – Piano Collection
00285510 ..... $19.99

Pirates of the Caribbean – Curse of the Black Pearl
00313256 ..... $22.99

Pride & Prejudice
00123854 ..... $17.99

Queen
00289784 ..... $19.99

John Williams Anthology
00194555 ..... $24.99

George Winston Piano Solos
00306822 ..... $22.99

MIXED COLLECTIONS

Beautiful Piano Instrumentals
00149926 ..... $19.99

Best Jazz Piano Solos Ever
00312079 ..... $27.99

Big Book of Classical Music
00310508 ..... $24.99

Big Book of Ragtime Piano
00311749 ..... $22.99

Christmas Medleys
00350572 ..... $16.99

Disney Medleys
00242588 ..... $19.99

Disney Piano Solos
00313128 ..... $17.99

Favorite Pop Piano Solos
00312523 ..... $17.99

Great Piano Solos
00311273 ..... $19.99

The Greatest Video Game Music
00201767 ..... $19.99

Most Relaxing Songs
00233879 ..... $19.99

Movie Themes Budget Book
00289137 ..... $14.99

100 of the Most Beautiful Piano Solos Ever
00102787 ..... $29.99

100 Movie Songs
00102804 ..... $32.99

Peaceful Piano Solos
00286009 ..... $19.99

Piano Solos for All Occasions
00310964 ..... $24.99

Sunday Solos for Piano
00311272 ..... $17.99

Top Hits for Piano Solo
00294635 ..... $16.99

HAL•LEONARD®

View songlists online and order from your favorite music retailer at
halleonard.com

Prices, content, and availability subject to change without notice.

Disney characters and artwork TM & © 2021 Disney